Big Panda
and
Tiny Dragon

JAMES NORBURY

在黑暗的日子裡，
陪伴是最溫暖的曙光

詹姆斯・諾柏瑞―著　　鄭煥昇―譯

謹以此書獻給每一個迷失的靈魂。

This book is dedicated to everyone who gets lost.

CONTENTS
目錄

春
SPRING

要勇敢。
你永遠不知道這場相遇會將我們帶往何處。

Be brave.

You never know what a
first meeting might lead to.

「新的一天跟新的開始，」
小小龍說，
「我們該做點什麼呢？」

'A new day and a new beginning,'
said Tiny Dragon.

'What shall we do with it?'

「哪一樣比較重要，」大熊貓問，「旅程或目的地？」
「旅伴比較重要，」小小龍說。

'Which is more important,' asked Big Panda,
'the journey or the destination?'

'The company,' said Tiny Dragon.

「我現在忙到沒空賞花，」小小龍說。
「那你才更應該賞花，」大熊貓說，
「花明天不一定還在。」

'I'm too busy to see the flowers right now,' said Tiny Dragon.

'All the more reason to look at them,' said Big Panda.
'And they might not be here tomorrow.'

「自然是不是很不可思議！」小小龍說。

「是，」大熊貓附和，

「但我們也是自然的一部分，就像樹與蜘蛛一樣，所以我們也同樣不可思議。」

'Isn't nature incredible!' said Tiny Dragon.

'It is,' agreed Big Panda.
'But we are just as much a part of nature
as the tree or the spider, and just as amazing.'

「大熊貓，」小小龍說，
「我喜歡你聽我說話、對我說話，還有伴我同行的方式，
但比起這些，我更喜歡你給我的感覺。」

'Big Panda,' said Tiny Dragon,
'I like the way you listen to me
and talk to me and travel with me,
but most of all, I like the way
you make me feel.'

「試著騰出時間來給小事情，」大熊貓說。
「小事情往往才最要緊。」

'Try to make time for the small things,'
said Big Panda.

'They are often the most important.'

「最要緊的事⋯⋯」大熊貓說，
「⋯是專心。」

'The most important thing . . .'
said Big Panda,

'. . . is to pay attention.'

「只因為你不知道自己在往哪去，不代表你就迷路了，」小小龍頗具深意地說。
「確實，」大熊貓答道，「但此刻的我們是真的迷路了。」

'Just because you don't know where you
are going, it doesn't mean you are lost,'
said Tiny Dragon profoundly.

'Very true,' replied Big Panda,
'but in this case we are definitely lost.'

「那棵樹真的是苦過來的，」小小龍說。

「沒錯，」大熊貓說，「但它依舊屹立不搖，而且出落得又強大，又美不勝收。」

'That tree has been through some rough times,'
said Tiny Dragon.

'Yes,' said Big Panda, 'but it's still here
and it has gained strength and beauty.'

「快點！」小小龍尖叫著。「我們有好多事要做！」
「河流一向不急不徐，」大熊貓說，
「即便一路上有重重阻礙，也從沒聽說它到不了目的地。」

'Hurry!' squeaked Tiny Dragon.
'There is so much to do!'

'The river doesn't hurry,' said Big Panda,
'yet despite many obstacles,
always gets where it's going.'

「什麼動靜都沒有。」小小龍說。
「也許，」大熊貓說，
「事情正在默默地醞釀。」

'Nothing is happening,' said Tiny Dragon.

'Maybe,' said Big Panda,
'it's happening underneath first.'

「有時候我覺得我不夠好，」小小龍說。

「櫻桃樹不會拿自己去跟其他的樹比較，它只是盡情開花，」大熊貓說。

'Sometimes I think I'm not good enough,'
said Tiny Dragon.

'A cherry tree doesn't compare itself
to other trees,' said Big Panda,
'it just blossoms.'

樹葉的各種用途：第一種——化爲一葉扁舟。

Uses for a leaf: no. 1 – a boat.

「有時候，你只是需要傻氣一點。」

'Sometimes, you just have to be silly.'

你在旅程中做的每個決定，都會帶領你更接近或更偏離目的地。

Each decision you make on your
journey takes you closer or further
from where you want to go.

「犯錯代表你在嘗試，」大熊貓說，
「不要放棄。」

'Mistakes mean you're trying,' said Big Panda.
'Don't give up.'

「我想要改變這世界，」小小龍說。
「就從需要你幫助的下一個人做起，」大熊貓說。

'I want to change the world,' said Tiny Dragon.

'Start with the next person who needs
your help,' replied Big Panda.

「地圖沒有顯示我應該去的地方，」小小龍說。
「你的旅程不會顯示在任何地圖上，」大熊貓說，
「你得去發掘自己的道路。」

'The map doesn't show
where I'm supposed to go,'
said Tiny Dragon.

'Your journey isn't shown
on any map,' said Big Panda.
'You must discover your own path.'

「我已經想念他了，」小小龍說。
「要是他受傷了怎麼辦？」
「你已經在他最需要的時候幫助過他了，」大熊貓說，
「說不定他長命百歲又幸福美滿？」

'I miss him already,' said Tiny Dragon.
'What if he gets hurt?'

'You helped him when he needed it most,'
said Big Panda,
'and what if he goes on to live a long
and happy life?'

「前路看起來很艱難，」大熊貓說。
「不論路變得多困難，」小小龍說，
「我們都會一起面對。」

'The path ahead looks difficult,' said Big Panda.

'No matter how hard it gets,' said Tiny Dragon,
'we'll face it together.'

「我希望此刻能夠化爲永恆，」小小龍說。
「這個瞬間就等於一切了，」大熊貓微笑說。

'I wish this moment could last forever,'
said Tiny Dragon.

'This moment is all there is,'
smiled Big Panda.

夏
SUMMER

什麼都不做，絕對不等於浪費時間。

Time doing nothing is never wasted.

「我能早點認識你就好了，」小小龍說，
「那樣我們就能一起踏上更多冒險了。」

'I wish I had met you earlier,'
said Tiny Dragon, 'so we could have gone
on even more adventures together.'

「我存在的意義是什麼？」小小龍說。
大熊貓頓了一拍說，「你存在是爲了在那塊石頭上坐著，陪伴你的朋友。」

'What is my purpose?' asked Tiny Dragon.

Big Panda paused, then said,
'To sit on that stone and be with your friend.'

「我的頭有時候就像這場風雨一樣狂亂，」小小龍說。
「認真傾聽，」大熊貓說，
「你會聽到雨滴打在石頭上的劈啪聲。
即便在風雨中，想找到一點平靜也不是不可能。」

'My head feels like this storm sometimes,'
said Tiny Dragon.

'If you really listen,' said Big Panda,
'you can hear the raindrops
splashing on the stone.
It's possible to find a little peace,
even in a storm.'

一隻堅持不放棄的小小龍，就會變大龍。

An Elder Dragon
is a Tiny Dragon
who never gave up.

GRANDPA DRAGON

（阿公龍）

「我們還有很長的路要走，」大熊貓說。

小小龍笑了，「阿公龍以前會說，『千里之行，始於一杯茶。』」

'We have a long way to go,' said Big Panda.

Tiny Dragon grinned. 'Grandpa Dragon used to say,
"A journey of a thousand miles begins with a cup of tea."'

「你是很好的聽眾，」小小龍說。
「聽人說話從沒讓我惹上麻煩，」大熊貓說。

'You're a good listener,' said Tiny Dragon.

'Listening has never landed me in trouble,'
replied Big Panda.

　　「我找不到適合的地方插這最後一枝花，」小小龍有點惱怒。
大熊貓若有所思地嚼著竹子，「就是不完美才讓它看起來如此完美。」

'I can't find the right place for this last branch,'
huffed Tiny Dragon.

Big Panda chewed his bamboo thoughtfully.
'It's the imperfections that make it perfect.'

「最適合拿來配茶的，」大熊貓說，
「就是好朋友。」

'The best thing to have with tea,'
said Big Panda, 'is a good friend.'

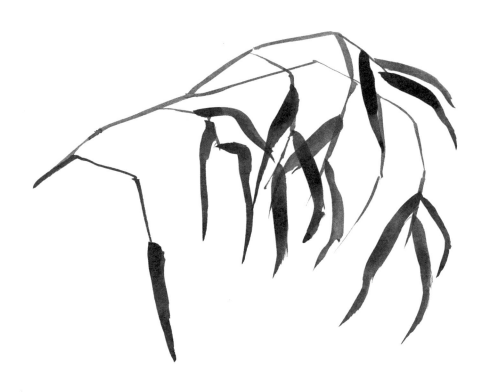

「我很擔心，」小小龍說，
「我不知道接下來要怎麼辦。」
「即便一下子也好，」大熊貓說，
「暫停、呼吸、聆聽風中的竹林。」

'I'm worried,' said Tiny Dragon.
'I don't know what to do next.'

'For just a moment,' said Big Panda,
'stop, breathe and listen to
the wind in the bamboo.'

「你在做什麼？」小小龍問。
「我也不知道，」大熊貓說，
　　「但很好玩就是了。」

'What are you doing?'
asked Tiny Dragon.

'I've no idea,' said Big Panda,
'but it's great fun.'

為別人製造幸福，
你可能會順便找到自己的。

If you seek happiness for others,
you may find it for yourself.

「你知道嗎，」小小龍說，
「現在可能就是將來我們會非常懷念的美好時光。」
「果真如此，」大熊貓說，
「那我們就永遠不要停止製造這些美好的回憶。」

'You know,' said Tiny Dragon,
'these might be the good old days that
we'll look back on with great longing.'

'In that case,' said Big Panda,
'let's never stop making them.'

愛，不需要解釋。

Love needs no explanation.

只要一起，我們就沒有做不到的事情。

Together, we can do anything.

有些人就像蠟燭。

他們徹底燃燒自己
是爲了替人創造光明。

Some people are like candles.

They burn themselves out
to create light for others.

葉子的第十七種用法：陽傘（跟晚餐）。

Uses for a leaf: no. 17 – a parasol (and dinner).

「快點，大熊貓，我們要遲到了！」
大熊貓坐了下來，
「我寧可想說我是在讓人們有所期待。」

'Hurry up, Big Panda,
we're going to be late!'

Big Panda sat down.
'I like to think I'm creating anticipation.'

「這座花園美極了，」小小龍說。
大熊貓點了頭，「要不是走錯路那麼多次，我們根本不會發現這地方。」

'This garden is beautiful,' said Tiny Dragon.
Big Panda nodded. 'And we only found it
because we went the wrong way so many times.'

「你好像都沒在做什麼事情，」
小小龍說。
「我這叫充滿潛力，」
大熊貓打起哈欠。

'You don't do much,'
said Tiny Dragon.

'I'm full of potential,'
yawned Big Panda.

秋
AUTUMN

「秋天一來，」大熊貓說，「冬天也不遠了。」
「喔喔⋯⋯」小小龍說，「那就有更多晚上可以舒服地在一起⋯⋯喝茶。」

'Autumn is here,' said Big Panda,
'and soon winter will be upon us.'

'Oooh . . .' said Tiny Dragon.
'More cosy evenings together . . . with tea.'

葉子的第六十二種用法：雨傘。

Uses for a leaf: no. 62 – an umbrella.

「我們又迷路了，」大熊貓說。

「迷路的時候，」小小龍說，

「我覺得有個不錯的辦法，就是回到原點去回想初衷。」

'We're lost again,' said Big Panda.

'When I'm lost,' said Tiny Dragon,
'I find it helps to go back to the beginning
and try to remember why I started.'

「要是遇到有人不喜歡我，或不喜歡我做的事，那該怎麼辦？」小小龍問。
「你要走自己的路，」大熊貓說，
「失去那些人，總比失去你自己好。」

'What if I meet people who don't like me
or the things I do?' asked Tiny Dragon.

'You must walk your own path,' said Big Panda.
'Better to lose them than lose yourself.'

「我的花⋯⋯」小小龍說。
「所有東西終將成為過去，小傢伙，所以它們才會如此寶貴。」

'My flower . . .' said Tiny Dragon.

'All things must come to pass, little one.
That's what makes them so precious.'

「要對所有人都好，並不容易，」小小龍說。
「確實，」大熊貓說，
「更難的是對自己好，但我們一定要試著這麼做。」

'It's hard being kind to everyone,' said Tiny Dragon.

'True,' said Big Panda, 'and hardest of all to be
kind to ourselves, but we must try.'

放手，或被拖著走。

Let go or be dragged.

喝茶的時候⋯⋯就喝茶。

When drinking tea . . . drink tea.

「你在想什麼？」小小龍問。
「沒什麼，」大熊貓說，
「一切都好。」

'What are you thinking about?'
asked Tiny Dragon.

'Nothing,' said Big Panda.
'It's wonderful.'

「我找不到出洞的路，」小小龍說。
大熊貓笑了，「那我就去洞裡坐著陪你。」

'I can't find my way out of this hole,'
said Tiny Dragon.

Big Panda smiled.
'Then I will come and sit in it with you.'

「葉子在凋落，」小小龍說。
「別難過，」大熊貓說，
「秋天，是大自然在告訴你放手可以有多美。」

'The leaves are dying,' said Tiny Dragon.
'Don't be sad,' said Big Panda.

'Autumn is nature's way of showing
us how beautiful letting go can be.'

「看我找到了什麼。」

'Look what I found.'

「一個嘗試新東西的機會，」大熊貓說。

'Oh,' said Big Panda,
'an opportunity to try something new.'

「你今天好安靜喔，」小小龍說。
大熊貓笑了，「我只是不覺得我的聲音會比雨聲悅耳。」

'You're quiet today,' said Tiny Dragon.

Big Panda smiled.
'I don't think I can improve on the sound of the rain.'

「這眞的行得通嗎？」

'I'm not sure this is working . . .'

「那棵樹怎麼還站得住？」小小龍問。

「趁著好天，」大熊貓說，

「它扎根扎得夠深，現在才什麼風暴都撐得過去。」

'How is that tree still standing?' asked Tiny Dragon.

'During better times,' said Big Panda, 'it grew deep roots.
Now it can weather any storm.'

「可惜我們沒趁很久以前就把這棵樹種下，」小小龍說。

「否則它現在會有多高大啊。」

「我們正在種下它啊，」大熊貓說，

「那才是最重要的。」

'It's a shame we didn't plant this tree a long time ago,'
said Tiny Dragon. 'Imagine how big it would be.'

'We're doing it now,' said Big Panda.
'That's the important thing.'

「你可以聽到林間的風聲嗎，小小龍？
那是大自然在告訴我們要花點時間停下腳步、好好呼吸，
什麼都不想。」

'Can you hear the wind in the trees, Tiny Dragon?

That's nature's way of telling us to take a moment
to stop, breathe and just be.'

「你對自己狠過嗎，大熊貓？」

大熊貓看著湖上的漣漪。

「我看著你是多麼溫柔，小小龍，我也試著用這股溫柔去對待自己。」

'Are you ever mean to yourself, Big Panda?'

Big Panda watched the ripples spread across the lake.

'I see how gentle you are, Tiny Dragon,
and try to treat myself with the same kindness.'

「這條路上有如此多的難關，」小小龍說。
「確實，」大熊貓也同意，
「但每個困難都讓我們學習到很多。
而且你想想，登頂之後的景色會有多美。」

'There have been so many difficulties along this path,'
said Tiny Dragon.

'There have,' agreed Big Panda, 'but we have
learned something from each one.

And imagine how good the view
will be when we reach the top.'

「不論別人讚美你還是批評你，小小龍，
都試著拿出風度去接受。
一棵樹要變強，需要經歷各式各樣的情境。」

'Whether people praise you
or criticize you, Tiny Dragon,
try to accept it gracefully.

It takes all kinds of conditions
to create a strong tree.'

傾聽，是你能替別人做的一件美事。

Listening to someone is one of the
greatest things you can do for them.

替人點亮提燈，
你也不知不覺照亮了自己的前路。

When you light a lantern
for someone else,
you cannot help but
light up your own path.

（你想要什麼？）

「不去嘗試，」大熊貓說，
「你永遠不會知道自己能不能飛。」

'If you don't try,' said Big Panda,
'you'll never know if you can fly.'

「我累了，」小小龍嘆道。
「累了就停下來歇會兒，」
大熊貓說，「喝杯茶配星星。」

'I'm tired,' sighed Tiny Dragon.

'Then it's time to stop,' said Big Panda,
'watch the stars and have a cup of hot tea.'

「你在慶祝什麼？」小小龍問。
「我在慶祝被雨淋，」大熊貓說，「跟你一起。」

'What are you celebrating?' asked Tiny Dragon.

'Getting rained on,' said Big Panda. 'With you.

「這蠟燭也太小了吧，」小小龍說。
「光明不論多小，」大熊貓笑道，
「都贏過一片黑暗。」

'That's a very small candle,' said Tiny Dragon.

'However small the light,' smiled Big Panda,
'it's better than darkness.'

「我想開一間攤子賣恐怖南瓜，」小小龍說，
「但我怕我會失敗。」
大熊貓給朋友添了些茶。
「你是有可能會失敗，小傢伙，
但如果你因為害怕而連試都不去試，
那你就鐵定會失敗。」

'I want to open a scary pumpkin stall,'
said Tiny Dragon, 'but I'm afraid I'll fail.'
Big Panda poured his friend some more tea.

'You might fail, little one, but if you let fear stop
you from even trying, failure is assured.'

有時候你能做的，就是替人泡杯茶。
對方需要的，也只是一杯茶。

Sometimes all you can do
is make someone a cup of tea.
It might be enough.

有些日子，
光起得了床就是打贏了一場仗。

There are days
when just getting up is a victory.

「宇宙是什麼？」小小龍問。
大熊貓仰望起夜空。
「宇宙就是我們，小傢伙。
我們就是深不見底的海洋跟夏季的閃電——沒有什麼比我們更令人嘆為觀止。」

'What is the Universe?' asked Tiny Dragon.

Big Panda looked up at the night sky.

'We are, little one. We are depthless oceans and summer
lightning – there is nothing more magnificent.'

冬
WINTER

「你已經揹著我好多天了，」小小龍說。
「往好處想，」大熊貓說，「至少不是小熊貓揹著大大龍。」

'You've been carrying me for so many days now,'
said Tiny Dragon.

'It could be worse,' said Big Panda.
'We could be Big Dragon and Tiny Panda.'

「每個季節都是獨立的存在，」大熊貓說，「又都各有神奇之處。」
「就跟我們一樣，」小小龍笑道。

'Each season is completely different,' said Big Panda,
'yet each has its wonders.'

'Just like us,' grinned Tiny Dragon.

有時候，
踏上不知道要去哪兒的旅程是好事一樁。

Sometimes, it's good to head out
with no idea where you're going.

「你怎麼有辦法堅持走下去？」小小龍問。
「有時候，」大熊貓說，「再小的一步都勝過原地踏步。」

'How do you keep going?'
asked Tiny Dragon.

'Sometimes,' said Big Panda,
'even the smallest step
is better than no step.'

「今天是一整年白天最短的一天，」小小龍說，「冬天真的來了。」
「白天最短就代表夜晚最長，」大熊貓說，
「而漫長的黑夜有它特有的神奇之處。」

'It's the shortest day,' said Tiny Dragon.
'Winter is truly upon us.'
'But also the longest night,' said Big Panda

'and that comes with its own wonders.'

「我放棄，」小小龍說。
「沒關係的，」大熊貓說，「我們明天再試就好。」

'I give up,' said Tiny Dragon.

'That's OK,' said Big Panda.
'We'll try again tomorrow.'

「今晚又冷又黑，」小小龍說。

「別擔心，小傢伙，」大熊貓說，「日出總會再來的。」

'It's cold and dark tonight,' said Tiny Dragon.

'Don't worry, little one,' said Big Panda.
'The sun will rise again.'

「你要是太辛苦，小傢伙，你可以告訴我。我很樂意幫忙。」

'If you're struggling, little one, you can tell me.

I want to help.'

「有壞念頭代表我是個壞人嗎？」小小龍問。
「不，」大熊貓說，「波浪不等於海洋，念頭也不等於心靈。」

'Do bad thoughts make me a bad person?' asked Tiny Dragon.

'No,' said Big Panda. 'The waves are not the ocean.
The thoughts are not the mind.'

「我好累喔，」小小龍說。

大熊貓停了下來。

「冬天就是自然會縮起來、休養生息、為新起點累積能量的時候。
我們也可以做一樣的事情，小傢伙。」

'I am so tired,' said Tiny Dragon.

Big Panda paused. 'Winter is a time when nature withdraws,
rests and gathers its energy for a new beginning.

We are allowed to do the same, my little friend.'

「我忘了許下新年新希望了，」小小龍嘆道。
「別擔心，小傢伙，」大熊貓說，
「要是你有想要改變的事情，現在開始也完全可以。」

'I forgot to make my New Year's resolution,'
sighed Tiny Dragon.

'Don't worry, little one,' said Big Panda.
'If there's something you want to change
you can start right now.'

「你的三個願望是什麼？」小小龍問。
大熊貓思索了一會兒。
「我們一起⋯⋯ 旅行⋯⋯在雨裡。」

'What would your three wishes be?'
asked Tiny Dragon.

Big Panda pondered a moment.
'Us together . . . travelling . . . in the rain.'

「俯拾皆有美景，」大熊貓說，「但有時要看見並不容易。」

'There is beauty everywhere,' said Big Panda,
'but sometimes it's difficult to see.'

葉子的第一一一種用法：雪撬。

Uses for a leaf: no. 111 – a sledge.

「我無法解釋自己的感覺，」小小龍說。
大熊貓笑了。
「沒關係，語言本來就對應不了萬事萬物。」

'I can't explain how I feel,'
said Tiny Dragon.

Big Panda smiled. 'That's OK.
Words are not adequate for all things.'

在我精疲力盡的時候，你給了我力量。

You give me strength when all mine has gone.

春
SPRING

破蛹而出之前，是蝴蝶最辛苦的時候。

Butterflies struggle most just before they emerge.

「你相信輪迴嗎？」小小龍問道。
大熊貓打了個哈欠。
「我相信每一天的每一分鐘，我們都可以放手並重新來過。」

'Do you believe in reincarnation?'
asked Tiny Dragon.

Big Panda yawned. 'I believe that
every minute of every day,
we can let go and start again.'

即便是遍體鱗傷的樹木，
也可以開出美不勝收的花朵。

Even a damaged tree can produce
the most beautiful blossoms.

「我們快到了嗎？」小小龍問。
大熊貓笑云，
「希望還沒有。」

'Are we nearly there yet?'
asked Tiny Dragon.

Big Panda smiled.
'I hope not.'

JAMES NORBURY

詹姆斯·諾柏瑞

藝術家、文字作者兼插畫家,詹姆斯是個身體力行的自然與動物愛好者。他大學主修動物系,生活中吃全素,當志工選的是非營利的英國貓咪保護協會,平日則與愛妻在英國南威爾斯照料七隻貓咪的起居。在空閒時喜歡閱讀、打電動、彈吉他,不然就是練練空手道。

Afterword
後記

之前我有過一段非常辛苦的時期，而就在當時，我邂逅了二手書店裡的一本佛教相關書籍。讀了之後的我在對內容感到驚豔之餘，也隨即開始鑽研靈性與修持。而在這樣的研究中愈有小成，我就愈意識到自己無需成為自身負面思想的奴隸。

在發現這些能大大增加我的幸福感之後，我決心要幫助別人。我加入了撒瑪利亞人（英國的張老師專線）的行列，開始接聽求助者的電話，了解他們是如何為孤獨、焦慮與憂鬱所苦。人間的苦難之多著實嚇到了我，也啓發了我想在身處的社區裡發起小小的支持團體，只可惜 COVID-19 的發生讓計畫只能暫停。

但山不轉路轉，我決定提起畫筆來傳遞這些強大而能改變人心的想法，用簡單易懂的方式使人們接收到這些訊息。一開始我也沒把握此舉究竟有沒有效果，但事實證明我收到了來自四面八方的聯繫，包括不同文化、宗教背景、國家與年齡層的讀者都想讓我知道一件事情：我的畫，幫助他們度過了難關。

所有的畫作都有我全心的投入，而我想那正是那些色彩與線條能觸動人心的原因——每一幅畫裡，都摻有我靈魂的碎片。

Acknowledgements

誌謝

本書，集合了我生活體驗之大成。我因此要向所有與我有過交集的人致意；是你們，共同塑造了今天的我，而沒有今天的我，就不會有今天的這本創作——所以，謝謝你們每一個人。

但話說回來，有些人對這本書的貢獻就是更多一些。

茹絲，她的存在對我就是一種幫助。她是我世界的中心，我每一天都愛她更多一點。

我的母親與父親，他們不僅教會了我要凡事靠自己，要懂得藝術作為理念傳達工具的重要性，還總是扮演我各種光怪陸離計畫的後盾。沒有他們在我的生命裡，我絕不可能相信藝術可以養活自己——所以謝謝你們。

我的兩位手足，艾倫與潔恩——你們總是在一旁鼓勵我，支持我。

盧多，你能替我賣出版權，真的是嚇到我了。我把信寄給了那麼多經紀人，惟一相信我的人是你。真是感激不盡。我希望你對我的信心可以得到回報。我自認自己不光是找了一個經紀人，更交到了一個朋友。還有伊芙，我知道妳在幕後做了多少事情——謝謝妳。

丹，我真的是走了運能認識你。我想像不到有其他編輯能跟我如此志同道合，或是能如此深刻理解我想要做的事情。我還想衷心感謝在企鵝出版的每一位同仁，因為我這本自得其樂的小繪本能走向世界，少不了你們辛勤的付出——安姬、碧依、莎拉、李、強、崔西、丹・P-B、芮貝卡、安潔莉、凡妮莎、蘇菲、艾莉與克莉絲提娜。

給在社群網路上追隨的粉絲：你們的支持與鼓勵是我能走到這一步的最大動力，謝謝你們。

給我在撒瑪利亞專線的同事：工作上總是有難熬的時候，但知道有彼此可以相互扶持，感覺天差地遠。能跟打進來的朋友在電話上交流，是我的榮幸，他們的故事對我的影響力，令我難以言喻。不過分地說，若沒有他們，就不會有這本書。

還有當然不能不提的是我的動物朋友——只不過偶爾我會納悶你們究竟是想療癒我，還是想把我逼瘋。

大人國 005

在黑暗的日子裡，陪伴是最溫暖的曙光

大熊貓與小小龍的相伴旅程

作者：詹姆斯・諾柏瑞（James Norbury） ｜譯者：鄭煥昇｜主編：陳家仁｜企劃：藍秋惠｜美術設計：陳恩安

總編輯：胡金倫｜董事長：趙政岷｜出版者：時報文化出版企業股份有限公司／108019台北市和平西路三段240號4樓／發行專線：02-2306-6842／讀者服務專線：0800-231-705；02-2304-7103／讀者服務傳真：02-2302-7844／郵撥：19344724時報文化出版公司／信箱：10899臺北華江橋郵政第99信箱／時報悅讀網：www.readingtimes.com.tw｜法律顧問：理律法律事務所　陳長文律師、李念祖律師｜印刷：華展印刷有限公司｜初版一刷：2022年1月14日｜初版十三刷：2024年9月16日｜定價：新台幣380元（缺頁或破損的書，請寄回更換）

ISBN 978-957-13-9725-2｜Printed in Taiwan

在黑暗的日子裡,陪伴是最溫暖的曙光：大熊貓與小小龍的相伴旅程／詹姆斯・諾柏瑞（James Norbury）著；鄭煥昇譯. -- 初版. -- 臺北市：時報文化出版企業股份有限公司，2022.01｜160面；17×20.8公分. --（大人國；005）｜譯自：Big panda and tiny dragon｜ISBN 978-957-13-9725-2（精裝）｜1.情緒 2.生活指導 176.5｜110019246